For my granddaughter, Jessica—NS

To my whole family—SB

♥   ♥   ♥

Library of Congress Cataloging-in-Publication
data is on file with the publisher.

Text copyright © 1976, 2016 by Norma Simon
Pictures copyright © 2016 by Sarah S. Brannen
Published in 2016 by Albert Whitman & Company
ISBN 978-0-8075-0286-0

Printed in China
10 9 8 7 6 5 4 3 2 1 LP 24 23 22 21 20 19 18 17 16 15

For more information about Albert Whitman & Company,
visit our web site at www.albertwhitman.com.

About This Book

More than forty years ago, this book introduced children to combinations of people who live together and are called a family. The concept has broadened since then to include more people as parents, brothers, and sisters in contemporary families. We hope the book will encourage children to talk about their own families and to discover the variety of people who fit under the big umbrella redefined as family.

Children forty years ago and children today still define family on the basis of their own experiences. Children still idealize adults in their family. Children still learn values by imitating attitudes and behaviors they observe. The supportive role of families and the child's place in the center of his or her world are reflected in this book. The new illustrations are of present-day people for present-day children.

Today nursery schools, prekindergartens, and day care centers are generally accepted as part of a child's education. We know that all children need emotional and physical lives nourished by love, trust, good nutrition, a sense of belonging, and support provided by the child's family and schooling. Our goal is to help each child grow into an adult who is self-assured, trusting, curious, creative, capable, healthy, and kind to other people. Children who grow up in positive, responsive environments thrive and survive through good times and troubled times. Family, relatives, friends, and good people of all ages matter very much in the lives of our children.

Norma Simon

A family is YOU and the people who live with you, love you, and take care of you. There are all kinds of families, but your own is the one you know best.

Families come in all sizes—big families, middle-sized families, little families. The people in a family are all ages too. Young families with young children, middle-aged families with teenaged children, and old families with grown-up children and grandchildren.

Families come with all kinds of people…different sizes,
different ages. Some people in families look like each other…
some look very different from each other. There are all kinds of families.

People who live together, love together, fight together, and make up
together, work and play with each other, laugh, cry, and live under
one roof…together…they are a family.

A family is people who belong together, like husbands and wives
and their children, like mothers and children…like fathers and children,
like grandparents and grandchildren who live together.

People in a family fit just right together,
like all the pieces in a puzzle.

What's special about a family? It's the feelings they have about each other from living together, sharing good times and bad times...growing together.

A family can be a mother, a father, and children growing up.

A family can be two mothers and their children.

A family can be two fathers and their children.

A family can be a mother and her children.

A family can be a father and his children, living, loving,

working, and sharing…a family.

When grandchildren and grandparents live together, they are a family.
When nieces and nephews live with aunts and uncles, they are a family.
Children need grown-ups who take good care of them.

People in a family may have different last names, but they are still
a family. A stepmother or a stepfather, stepbrothers or stepsisters,
they are all part of your family.

Do you have any stepsisters or stepbrothers? You can be a stepbrother or a stepsister to other people in your family. Did you know that?

A big sister or a big brother taking care
of younger children…they are a family.
A father and mother together, their children
grown up and away from home…
they are a family too.

Families like to come together for holidays, birthdays, and weddings, for happy times and sad times. When families get together they talk a lot, they eat a lot, and they laugh out loud a lot. When everyone has said good-bye, the house feels…empty.

Family people have family names like father, mother, sister, brother, daughter, son, cousin, uncle, aunt, niece, and nephew. Some families have special names they call their grandmothers and grandfathers. What do you call your grandma and grandpa? Do you have special names for them?

When families get together, they hear many family names. Some children have a large number of relatives, too many to remember. Some children have a small number of relatives and it's easy to name every one. Can you name some of your aunts? Your uncles? Your grandparents? Do you know what their first names are?

YOU are part of your family, the caring
and the sharing and, especially, the loving.
From when you were a baby to when
you're a kid, and from when you're a
grown-up and for as long as you live,
YOU are always part of your family.

A family is YOU and the people who
live with you. They are one part of your
family. Some people in your family live
in different places. They are part of your
family too. Part of your family may live
far away…in another city…in another part
of town…or nearby, in a different house.

You visit them. They visit you.
And you know they are family people:
cousins and aunts and uncles and
grandparents are part of one big family.

A mother or father may live in a
different house, not with their children.
No matter how near or far away they live,
they are still part of the family.

Some families live in the same house
for a very long time. Other families
move often, from one house to another.
They take their special things with them,
like family pictures, a favorite chair,
books…pets…toys, important things.

When YOU are a grown-up, you can have
your own family, a new family…a young family.
When parents adopt or give birth to a child,
a new family begins.

The new family becomes part of the old ones:
part of the father's family,
part of the mother's family,
and both families grow bigger.

Families last a long…long…time.
New babies are born or adopted.
Some people die.

There are new husbands, new wives…

coming together and growing apart.

There are changes, but families go on.

Families share special stories that family
people like to tell and family people like to hear.
The stories belong to the whole big family.

Does your family tell stories? Do they tell any stories
about you? Something you said, something you did?
Maybe you hear the same stories over and over.
Someday…you'll tell them too.

Sometimes people in a family hardly see each other...
maybe it's because they live too far away, or maybe
it's because the family argues with one another.
Maybe people are working all the time and
they have no time to get together.

But when a family does come
together you hear them say:
"Oh, how the children have grown!"
"Your hair is still so curly..."
"Isn't it good to be together again?"
"I'd know your kids anywhere.
I remember when you looked like that."
Their family feelings keep people close,
like a strong, invisible circle.

When you need help, your family helps you.

When your family needs help, you help them.

People in a family help one another.

They try to take care of each other.

Yes, families are for caring…
for loving and sharing…
near or far, big or small…
all kinds of families.

Your family is always part of YOU.

YOU are always part of your family.

Families are special,

all kinds of families.